A HISTORY OF WORDS

FOR CHILDREN

MARY RICHARDS

A HISTORY OF WORDS

FOR CHILDREN

ILLUSTRATED BY Rose Blake

CONTENTS

INTRODUCTION

In this history of words, we'll think about what words are, and the way we use them. We'll look at how we use words to speak to each other, write stories and record the past. We'll discover the way our ancient ancestors used language and began writing words down— and the tools they had to invent in order to do it. We will also explore how technology has changed the way people communicate with each other over the years—from the invention of paper and printing, to the creation of the smartphone. As you read through the book, you'll discover many writers, inventors, scientists and speakers who do wonderful things with words. You'll meet people from throughout history, from the Akkadian princess *Enheduanna*, whose poems were written on the walls of a Sumerian temple 5,000 years ago, to the American *Lin-Manuel Miranda*, whose rhymes are performed in theaters around the world today.

I'm Mary, the author, and I love putting words together to make sentences, chapters and whole books like this one! I like reading words, too, especially the ones written by authors whose books I've enjoyed since I first learned to read.

Some of the people we'll meet on this journey are famous—and others are a complete mystery! Pictured above is a woman holding a stylus (an early pen made from a reed) and a tablet (a wax-coated pocket-book used for writing). We're lucky that this portrait still survives, because it was found in the ruins of the Italian city of Pompeii, which was destroyed when the great volcano Vesuvius erupted thousands of years ago. Some scholars believe that this might be a portrait of the Greek poet Sappho, but we don't know for certain—all we can really tell is that this is someone who loved writing.

If you'd like to look at what happened when, the timeline on page 90 will give you a quick guide to some of the important dates in our *History of Words*. You can also look up any words you don't know in the glossary on page 92. As you read through the book, you'll also see our illustrator, Rose Blake, exploring the pages—just like you, she's looking forward to meeting all the great wordsmiths. So, let's begin!

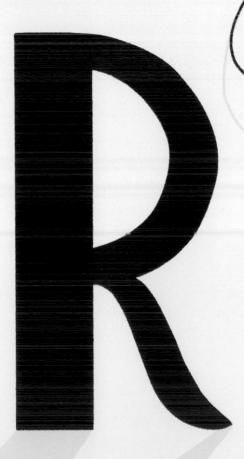

I'm Rose and I'm the illustrator of this book. Growing up, I lived across from a library and I used to walk to school with my head buried in a book! I like drawing pictures to help explain the words on the page.

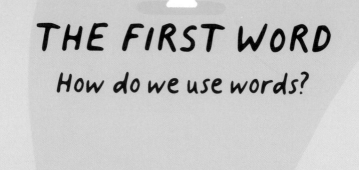

THE FIRST WORD
How do we use words?

I'm a blue whale. I talk to my friends using a range of deep, groaning sounds— and they can sometimes hear me up to 1,000 miles away!

Words and Communication

Do you have a favorite word? Is there a word you use more than any other? Every day, we use words to speak, read and write. With words, we can explain what we're thinking, and we can understand what our friends are saying to us, too. We can pick one or two short words to get someone's attention, or we can use some of the many thousands of words we know to tell a long story.

ONCE UPON A TIME, IN A LAND MUCH LIKE THIS ONE, THERE LIVED A WISE OLD OWL AND AN INQUISITIVE YOUNG BOOKWORM...

As humans, we're not alone in speaking—or communicating—with each other, but we are rather special. Animals communicate in amazing ways, but not in quite the way humans do. There are blue whales, who "speak" to each other over thousands of miles of ocean using pulsing and moaning sounds. Closer to home, my clever chicken Chuckle once appeared at the kitchen window squawking an alarm call. She wanted to let us know that we'd left her coop open, and that her friends were loose in the garden. She passed on her message successfully—and we put the hens back in their home safely. What a great communicator! But even Chuckle couldn't give a speech, write a book or search for instructions online!

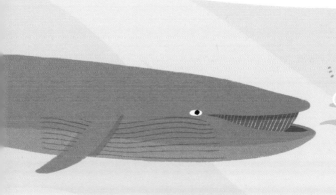

Speaking allows humans to describe, understand and make sense of the world around us. And unlike whales or chickens, we have also invented a way of writing words down. Words help us travel across time! The oldest surviving pieces of writing are around 5,500 years old. Written on ancient clay tablets, pieces of parchment and pages of books are tales of how our ancestors lived, what they believed and the stories they created. With words we can record important events and pass on ideas and stories to the people of the future. Every time we speak or write, we are adding our own words to a story that began all those thousands of years ago.

The Beginning of Language

Over thousands of years humans developed a unique way of communicating with each other. Today, there are over 7,000 different languages spoken across the world. But how did language begin? And why? Did it start among just one group of people, or did it take off in many different places at the same time? Scholars studying evolution are very interested in these questions. No one knows the first word ever spoken, or exactly how the grunts and gestures of our distant ancestors turned into speech that we recognize. But it's fun to imagine them using sounds or words to communicate "danger" ("There's a predator approaching!") or to get one another's attention. Most people agree that language developed very slowly. Historians like **Yuval Noah Harari** (b. 1976) have described how, by talking to each other, humans had a better chance of surviving in harsh conditions. They could team up to create the stone tools they needed to hunt wild animals and to farm the land. As time went on, the stories they told bonded them together and gave them a sense of belonging.

To work out how language began, scientists look for evidence. They listen to the thousands of languages that are spoken today, looking for clues as to how people communicated in the past. They study our ancestors' bones and the ancient objects they made. They also study the DNA and brains of today's humans and our closest animal relatives to see how different or similar we are. Modern scientists can study tiny strands of human DNA and scan brains using powerful computers that show which areas are fired up when people speak, read and write.

Born to Talk

Our brains and bodies are designed so that, from a very young age, we try to communicate with others. We might do this by making and copying sounds, creating different facial expressions or using our body movements to get across what we are thinking and feeling. Most importantly, we also use our brains to interpret and understand those actions. Let's think about the way many babies learn to talk. In the first weeks of their life they will make a few different noises, which might at first sound like nonsense. But by the age of 2 or 3 they are able to put together strings of words and even talk in sentences. Put together, these groups of sounds and words make a language.

Languages can sound very different, and speakers around the globe use their mouths, tongues and throats in different ways—from click languages like Xhosa (which is one of many languages spoken in South Africa—it includes a series of "clicking" sounds) to European languages like German (whose "rolled" "R" is produced in the back of the mouth). But wherever we live on the planet, the way we learn language is the same. Our neurons (the tiny electronic messengers in our brains) fire up and make new connections and pathways. As we'll go on to discover later in this book, the skills of reading and writing were invented many, many years later after humans learned to speak—and they take a little longer to master. Still, by the time we are 7 or 8 years old, we can usually recognize hundreds of characters and words. Fast forward ten years, and we are able to understand even trickier texts and ideas. In fact, our flexible human brains are designed so that we never stop learning.

Movements and Meaning

Have you ever read a message that someone has sent you—maybe an email or a text—and been confused about what the writer means? That's because people communicate in many ways. Facial expressions, gestures and tone are all important for passing on meaning. A smile, a frown or a wink can help explain what we're saying. The tone of our voice, the look on our face or whether we go up or down in pitch at the end of the sentence all help to make sense of the words we are using.

There are five senses—sight, hearing, touch, taste and smell. People often communicate using a combination of these, but we don't need them all. *Helen Keller* (1880–1968) was born in Alabama, USA, and became deaf and blind after a childhood illness. She learned to communicate using her sense of touch, spelling out signs and, later, words on the palm of her hand. Helen also learned to speak by touching the lips of other speakers, and she learned to read Braille, a system of writing and reading designed in the 1820s. It uses raised dots that are felt by the reader. Helen went to Harvard University and eventually wrote many books herself.

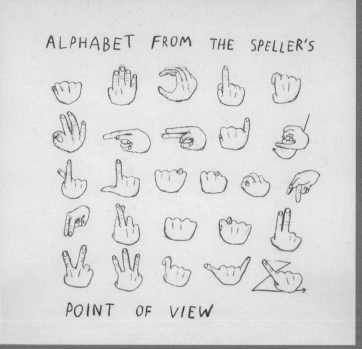

CHRISTINE SUN KIM, *Alphabet from the Speller's Point of View*, 2019.
[In American Sign Language]

American artist *Christine Sun Kim* (b. 1980) is known for her drawings, performances and installations. She was born Deaf and uses sign language to communicate. Sign language combines hand shapes, combinations and movements with other modifications (such as position and facial expression) and is a language with its own grammar. There are specific signs for most words and phrases, but individual letters are sometimes used to finger-spell words. Her work *Alphabet from the Speller's Point of View* (2019) shows the 26 American Sign Language letter signs from her perspective as she is signing, rather than from the perspective of the person she's communicating with. ASL (American Sign Language) is one of around 300 sign languages used in the world today.

17

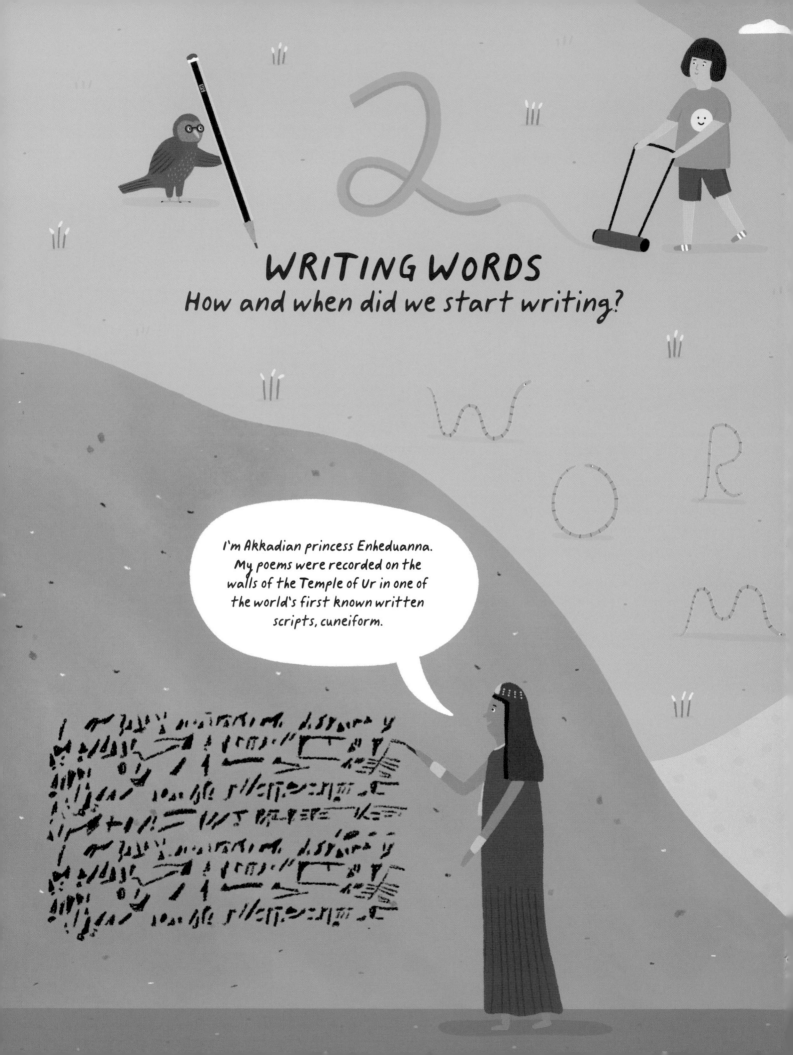

WRITING WORDS
How and when did we start writing?

I'm Akkadian princess Enheduanna. My poems were recorded on the walls of the Temple of Ur in one of the world's first known written scripts, cuneiform.

Telling Stories

Many thousands of years before writing was invented, stories were passed on by word of mouth. Around campfires and in caves, our ancestors told tales of heroes and adventurers; of how the world was created; and of characters who learned lessons about what was right and wrong. Stories can be very helpful! If you're having a bad time, a hopeful story can make you feel better. If you're thinking of behaving badly, a story might make you change your mind. Sharing stories brought people together back then, just as they do today.

Stories were told and re-told as people moved around the globe. For thousands of years, they weren't written down at all. The ancient Greek adventures the *Iliad* and the *Odyssey*, by **Homer**, were told long before they were finally recorded in the 8th century BCE. One theory is that the Greek alphabet itself (invented at around the same time) was created in order to preserve these epic tales.

You might be surprised at the age of some of the stories on your own bookshelf! Scholars have traced the fairy story of Cinderella, made famous by the *Brothers Grimm* (Jacob 1785–1863 and Wilhelm 1786–1859) in 1812, right back to a 2,000-year-old Greek tale of Rhodopis, a servant girl who marries a Pharaoh after her foot fits a golden sandal. In a Chinese version of the tale, told around 860 CE, hardworking girl Xe Yian is transformed by magic into a beautiful princess, and loses her shoe at a party. Could these stories have started as one original tale? Or is the dream of becoming a prince or princess so powerful that it was invented over and over again, in different times and lands?

The First Writing

The invention of writing changed the world! But it happened slowly, over many years. You're reading this now (or perhaps someone is reading it to you), using skills that your ancestors took tens of thousands of years to develop.

Across the world, archaeologists have found many different examples of early writing. The first marks—some over 30,000 years old—were etched in stone and painted on cave walls, among drawings of bison and other animals. In China, writing has been discovered on ancient tortoiseshells and animal bones. They are known as "oracle bones" because they were used to predict the future. The marked bones were put in a fire in a special ceremony, and any cracks that appeared were deciphered. Some ancient marks weren't even written by hand— in South America, the Incas recorded information on knotted strings called quipus.

This clay tablet was created more than 4,000 years ago by the Sumerians, an ancient people living in the region between the Tigris and Euphrates rivers, in modern day Iraq and Syria. It's written in a script called cuneiform—one of the earliest scripts that we are able to translate today. The little symbols were pressed into wet clay with a reed pen. To us now, they look mysterious and strange—and that's how they would have looked to many people at the time, too. Not everyone could read, and writing was done by trained scribes, who learned their craft in special schools. The text here isn't particularly exciting. It just records how many goats and sheep there were. Like many early scripts, the text is written in vertical columns, from right to left.

Tablet written in cuneiform, used to record numbers of goats and sheep

23

Sound Signs

Cuneiform wasn't just used to record facts and figures. Over hundreds of years its marks changed shape and turned into a script that looked much more like modern letters. Eventually, writers like the Akkadian princess **Enheduanna** (2285–2250 BCE) composed whole texts in cuneiform. Enheduanna even "signed" a set of poems, inscribed on the wall of the Temple of Ur, with her own signature mark— which some believe makes her one of the first ever recorded authors.

Around the same time as the Sumerians, the Egyptians were also writing and carving on the walls of their palaces and tombs. The first hieroglyphs appeared around 3200 BCE. Egyptian scribes later wrote on papyrus, a type of paper made from the reeds that grew next to the River Nile. Although at first glance hieroglyphs look like pictures, they are actually a detailed language that mixes pictures, symbols and sounds.

An ancient box from the tomb of Tutankhamun

Scholars enjoy discussing how all these early marks and signs turned into writing as we know it today. They agree that, very gradually, logograms (pictures representing things; for instance, a picture of a goat, or the moon) were replaced with phonograms (symbols that stood for sounds; such as the letters g-o-a-t, or m-o-o-n). Since cracking the code (see page 68), scholars know that this box from the tomb of the young Pharaoh *Tutankhamun* (who reigned from c. 1333–1323 BCE) spells out his name in a mix of "picture" and "sound" signs.

Today, some languages still mix picture characters and letter sounds. Children learning Chinese must learn to write several thousand logograms in order to master the language—they don't just use phonics or letter sounds. For example, in written Chinese, the word "angry" is made up of two characters—"fire" and "big."

Can you invent your own language? Grab a piece of paper and jot down some ideas!

蟲

貓頭鷹

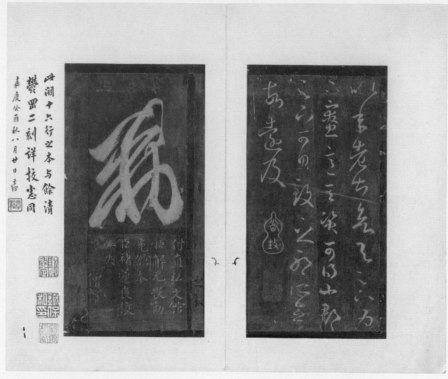

WANG XIZHI, *On the Seventeenth Day*

Super Scripts

Some experts can turn lettering into great works of art. Over in China in the 4th century CE, famous calligraphers like *Wang Xizhi* (303–361 CE) spent decades studying and copying the many thousands of Chinese characters. With brushes made of fine animal hair, calligraphers could make a huge range of strokes—thin, thick, straight or gracefully curved. Characters had to be drawn in a particular way, with each stroke made in the correct order—all learned from a teacher.

While Chinese contains thousands of symbols, some scripts contain much fewer characters. One of the earliest of these was the Greek alphabet, created in around 800 BCE, which had just 24 letters.

Α Β Γ Δ Ε Ζ
Η Θ Ι Κ Λ Μ
Ν Ξ Ο Π Ρ Σ
Τ Υ Φ Χ Ψ Ω

A thousand or more cuneiform or hieroglyph symbols had to be learned in the Egyptian and Sumerian systems, so the Greek system made writing—and reading—much easier. Greek philosopher Socrates even complained that writing would ruin people's powers of memory!

Many scripts are particularly striking when written by hand. Some handwritten scripts are so beautiful in message and appearance, many believe them to come directly from God. From the beginning of Islam in the 7th century CE, Arabic script was formed in elaborate, decorative characters and could only be written by trained experts. It was made with a flexible reed pen dipped in ink, which could create precise dots but also flowing, looping lines. Important messages from the Qur'an were written on holy buildings, where they blended in with striking geometric patterns. We'll learn more about religious texts on page 36.

From Tablet to Tablet—Writing Tools

We're still reading the words scratched into bones by the Chinese, baked into clay by the Sumerians, or carved in stone by the Romans. Some texts written on parchment (an early kind of paper made from stretched animal skins) have survived for thousands of years. Like a tattoo, ink etched into skin can't be rubbed out—it's indestructible! The Mayans of South America used jaguar skin to cover their books.

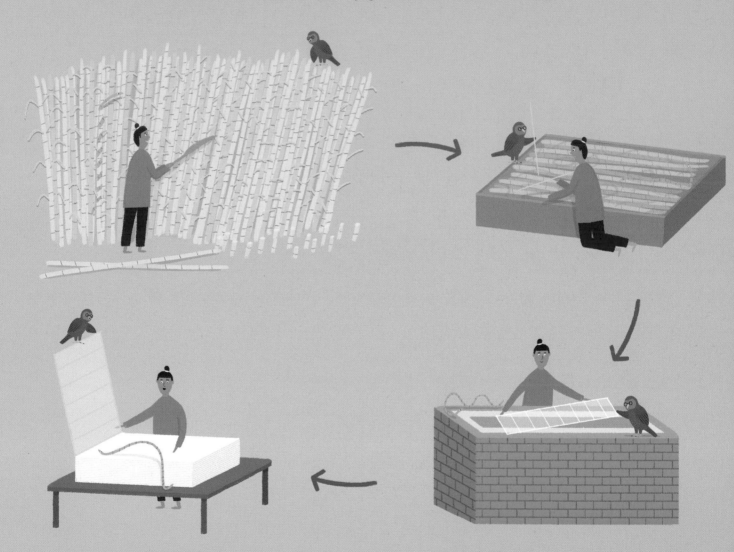

Paper—as we know it today—was invented in China around 100 CE. It was made from the crushed bark of the mulberry tree mixed with rags and water. For years, the recipe was a closely guarded secret, but by the 8th century CE the art of paper making had spread to South Asia and the Middle East; soon, book stalls and libraries were filled with thousands of scrolls and manuscripts.

It's funny to think that many of the tools used for writing in the
past have the same names as the electronic ones we use in our
homes today. There's a "tablet"—in ancient times, a piece of stone
or clay—which is also the name we give to the smart device we play
games, watch TV, draw and read on. Sometimes these are operated
by a "stylus"—a pen named after the hard reeds used to write on
parchment and papyrus. Our modern fountain pens are based on early
quills, made from feathers, whose hollow stalks served as a great place
to store ink. At school, you might use pencils or ballpoint pens—but so
many writers today create their work sitting typing at a keyboard. Do
you think the documents and messages we write on computers—stored
in hard drives or in "the cloud"—will last as long as the texts written on
clay, bones and stone in the past? Let's hope so!

READING WORDS
Who reads what is written?

I'm King Ashurbanipal, creator of one of the great libraries of the ancient world. In its ruins, archaeologists found one of the earliest surviving stories—the *Epic of Gilgamesh*.

The First Readers

Most of us start to speak in the first year of our lives, and talking comes quite naturally. But reading is tricky and takes much longer to conquer. It has to be learned slowly and carefully—whatever language we happen to speak—whether it's Mandarin, English, Arabic or Russian. If you're reading this now, give yourself a huge pat on the back!

The first readers didn't read books, of course. They "read" pictures, symbols and other marks, which were designed to remind them how much they'd paid for their goats, or who owned a particular field. As we've seen, the idea of a complete written language—as we know it today—was soon found across the ancient world. But only a small number of people in ancient societies could actually read. They didn't need to. From Greece to China, reading, like writing, was done by scholars and scribes. A scribe's job was to read aloud, as well as copy things down—and for a few thousand years, texts were mostly designed to be read out in public. In fact, the idea of silent reading—reading for pleasure, on your own—only became popular in the 19th century, a time when more and more people across the world were learning to read.

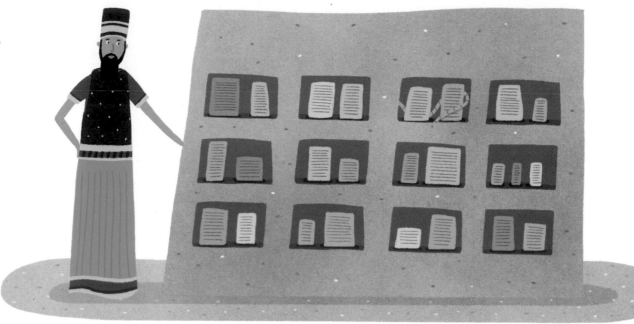

A House for Books

As cities got bigger, and people traded with their neighbors, there was much more of a need for writing—and reading. In fact, our ancestors produced so much text—on clay tablets, scrolls of papyrus and parchment—they had to work out how to store it all. In ancient times, as now, the place for collecting and storing important texts was the library. The Assyrian *King Ashurbanipal* (who reigned from 668–c. 627 BCE) had a library in the great city of Nineveh, which contained over 30,000 tablets written in cuneiform. One of the earliest surviving written stories—the 4,000-year-old *Epic of Gilgamesh*—was discovered here.

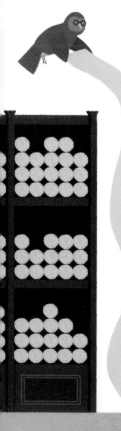

In Egypt, the Great Library of Alexandria—the largest library of the ancient world (founded around 285–246 BCE)—is said to have held hundreds of thousands of papyrus scrolls. Any ship that arrived in the port was forced to declare its books, which were then taken to the library, copied by scribes, and added to the collection. This was organized by subject into categories like medicine or poetry. Scrolls were arranged in (Greek) alphabetical order, from alpha to omega. As well as being homes for important texts, places like the House of Wisdom in Baghdad or the great libraries of Timbuktu became centers of learning. Scholars gathered there to share knowledge and teach students; they collected, translated and studied texts from all over the region.

New York Public Library, 1911

Of course, we still collect and store books today! By law, every single book that's published (including this one) enters the collections of the largest libraries in the world. The British Library in London is the world's largest. It has over 13 million books in its collection, and needs 460 miles of shelving to store them all—much of it underground! The libraries you visit in your cities or towns won't be as cavernous as the big libraries of Paris, New York or Shanghai! But whatever the library's size, librarians do everything they can to keep them well-stocked with books and open to everyone.

St George Slays the Dragon, from *Book of Hours,* 15th century

Holy Books

Writing spread across the ancient world, and many of the first texts written down were religious. Scribes and monks transferred onto papyrus, parchment and paper the holy words of God as delivered to Muhammad (the Qu'ran); epics of the Hindu gods like Krishna, Rama and Sita (the Mahabharata and the Ramayana); stories of Abraham, Moses and Noah (the Bible); or the philosophical writings of Lao-Tzu (the Tao Te Ching). These texts were copied and studied with great care and attention in temples, monasteries and libraries. From the Dead Sea Scrolls, the oldest surviving religious text (408 BCE–318 CE), to the earliest known book, the Buddhist Diamond Sutra (868 CE), it was texts themselves that began to be worshipped—for the words written within them were believed to have been sent directly from God.

Books—made from parchment (animal skins), bound between leather covers—allowed these holy words to travel far and wide. Illuminated manuscripts like the *Book of Kells* (9th century CE) and, later, small books of Christian prayers known as *Books of Hours*, were one-of-a-kind; painstakingly and expensively decorated and illustrated. It took a monk in a monastery over a year to copy out a Bible. This was slow, careful work. The lines had to be spaced out very neatly on the fine, valuable parchment.

How many words do you think there are in this book? Can you guess? A scribe would be able to look at a page and tell you exactly how long it would take them to copy it out!

Unlike scrolls, which had to be unfolded, books were designed for readers. They were small enough for one person to manage—resting on a lectern or held in the hand. They also had space around the text—called margins—into which these new readers could make their own notes.

In Print

The next huge change in our history of words was the
invention of printing. With printing, many copies of a single text could
be produced at once. It all began in China. From around 800 CE, text and
illustrations were carved by hand into wooden blocks, which were then
layered with ink. Sheets of paper (made from the bark of the mulberry
tree, see page 28) were pressed against them, and the loose pages
bound together. The text had to be carved in reverse, as if reflected in
a mirror. Beginning in the courts of Song Dynasty China (960–1269 CE),
for the first time in world history, books became widely popular. As well
as reading classics like the teachings of the Buddha, people came to
love histories, poetry and stories of the country's ruling families.

In the German city of Mainz in the 1440s everything changed again when **Johannes Gutenberg** (d. 1468) invented the printing press. With this, pages were "set" with individual metal letters or "type," which could be moved around into different combinations. With this method, thousands of copies of books could be printed at once. The Bible was the first book to be printed in this way, and it was a bestseller! Gutenberg's Bible was printed in Latin, in a script that looked a lot like the old handwritten version; only experts could read that, but later editions (like Martin Luther's version, translated into German in 1534), could be read by many more people. To date, it's estimated that more than 5 billion copies of the Bible have been printed in over 700 languages.

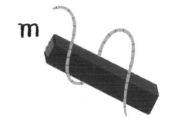

Gutenberg's press started a revolution. Soon, everyone wanted books! Italian **Aldus Manutius** (c. 1450–1515) began printing pocket-sized editions of Greek and Roman classic texts in 1490—which were a roaring success. It wasn't just books that were in print. Newspaper bulletins, pamphlets and posters, which could be printed quickly, also sprang up across cities. More books, and more text on the streets—of course—led to more readers!

ONCE UPON A TIME...

Reading Stories

What stories do you like reading? Do you like tales where characters go on an epic adventure? Fantastical stories where animals speak and humans have magical powers? Or perhaps you prefer real-life tales set in an actual historical place?

For centuries, and in lands across the world, stories have started with phrases like: "Once Upon A Time..." or "A Long Time Ago..." These words tell the reader that they must leave behind what they know, and get ready to enter a new, exciting world. When we open a book and start reading, we bring our own experiences with us. We think of all the stories we've ever read, and compare the lives and actions of the story characters with our own. This is what makes every book different for every reader.

GO! GO! GO!

Scholars have noticed that many of the world's most popular stories have quite a similar structure. The plots of some popular stories can be traced right back to one of the first recorded stories, the 4,000-year-old *Epic of Gilgamesh*—which tells of the adventures of the hero-king of Uruk as he searches for the secret of eternal life. One scholar, **Joseph Campbell** (1904–1987), wrote a book that explored myths and legends from around the world, and noted what they all shared—the journey of a hero and their return with new insights or powers. He called it *The Hero With A Thousand Faces* (1949). Inspired by that book, **George Lucas** (b. 1944) used its ideas to write a pretty famous film script—*Star Wars*.

Can you think of any other books that tell stories of heroes, quests and returns? Maybe you'll write one yourself, one day.

4

LEARNING WORDS
What is language?

I'm William Shakespeare. I wrote plays in 16th- and 17th-century England. I invented hundreds of words that went on to become part of the English language, including "gossip," "lonely" and "zany."

Speaking My Language

It is estimated that there are over 7,000 languages spoken around the world today—and even more that existed long ago! Why so many? Languages sprang up in different parts of the world and developed in their own way. In time, they spread across the globe. Over thousands of years, communities invented new words and formed different ways of pronouncing old ones. Languages also mixed together in a fascinating way. This paragraph contains words that come from Greek, Latin, German and French. Can you guess which ones? You can turn to page 93 to find out!

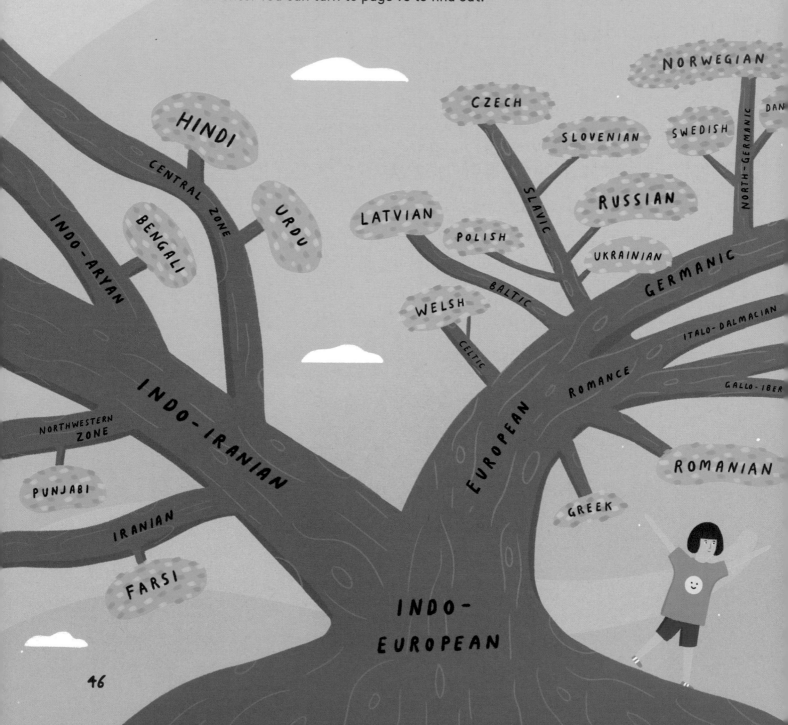

Linguists study our world's languages and group them into "family trees." This is a useful way of showing how they are all connected. Many languages from the same region can be grouped together. Around one third of the world's languages can be found in Africa, whose "tree" branches off into six separate families. In the biggest group are the languages that have been spoken in the area around the Niger and Congo rivers for at least 15,000 years. Over in Scandinavia, the Danish, Swedish and Norwegian languages are closely related, but Finnish is on a different tree entirely—in fact, it can be traced right back to a language spoken in the Ural mountains of Russia around 10,000 years ago.

Spoken and written languages are not always the same. The languages of China, including Mandarin and Cantonese, are all written down using the same script, but when spoken they are completely different. On the other hand, the Hindi and Urdu languages of India sound very similar to each other, but are written very differently—Hindi in Devanagari letters and Urdu in the Nastaliq script. Even people who speak exactly the same language have very different accents! Do you pronounce your words in the same way as your friends? Next time you're all talking together, listen carefully!

ENGLISH

U-FRISIAN

EST GERMANIC

ITALIAN

CATALAN

HIGH GERMAN

SWISS GERMAN

BERO-ROMANCE

LOW FRANCANIAN

FLEMISH

PORTUGUESE

AFRIKAANS

GERMAN

FRENCH

SPANISH

DUTCH

FINNISH

HUNGARIAN

STONIAN

This illustration shows some—but not all—of the Indo-European and Finno-Ugric languages, and the way they connect on their "family trees."

FINNO-UGRIC
URALIC

47

A World of Words

Your "first language" or "mother tongue" is the one you learned as a child when you started to talk. Mandarin Chinese, spoken by over 1.1 billion people, is the world's most common first language. English—with over 1.3 billion speakers—is the most widely spoken if you count people who use it as a second language. Some people speak many languages, such as the ancient Queen *Cleopatra* (who reigned from 51–30 BCE), who is believed to have been able to chat in nine languages including Greek, Egyptian and Arabic.

No matter how different languages are from each other, there are things they all share. Each has its own set of rules, or "grammar," that explains the way words should be used. One of the earliest known scholars of language, the Indian writer *Panini*, wrote a book about the Sanskrit language, in which he explained its words and sentences in detail.

Your name is something that you'll have whatever language you speak. Today, most people have a first name and a family name (often called a last name), passed down through the generations. Our ancestors found last names useful to identify people! Names often described jobs—like, in English, Baker. They referred to the place a person's from, like the Japanese Yamamoto ("bottom of the mountain"). Or, they described looks or personality—in Xhosa, Buhle ("beautiful"), in Hindi, Singh ("lion").

Names that meant "son of" were also very popular (in Spanish, Rodriguez is "son of Rodrigo," in Russia, Dimitrov is "son of Dimitri"). Today, in countries such as Iceland or Malaysia, families do not share last names—their names work in a different way. Let's say the Icelandic father is called Olaf; his son might be Magnus Olafsson (meaning Olaf's son), and his daughter Helga Olafsdóttir (meaning Olaf's daughter). But Magnus's son, Jón, would be Jón Magnusson (meaning Magnus's son)—and so it would go on.

Can you work out which groups the names of your friends fit into?

Organizing Words

Lists of words and their meanings have been found on clay tablets from over 4,000 years ago. Soon, books were used for organizing and recording language. Today, we're used to dictionaries being in alphabetical order, but that wasn't always the case. The Eyra, created in China around 200 BCE, included definitions of Chinese words and was organized by theme. But the first Arabic language dictionary Kitab al-'Ayn, compiled in Basra, Iraq, around 700 CE, arranged words according to the way they were pronounced.

Later books, like the English dictionary compiled by *Samuel Johnson* (1709–1784) in 1755, included notes on the history of words, quoting texts by authors like *William Shakespeare* (1564–1616). In the USA in 1828, *Noah Webster* (1758–1843) published his American dictionary with simpler ways of spelling some English words, such as "colour," which he changed to "color," and "centre," which he changed to "center." This spelling took off in America and is still used today.

A dictionary is a great way to learn new words. Have you ever played the dictionary game with friends? Choose an unusual word at random and write down some made-up definitions. Next, someone who hasn't seen the word reads out all the definitions, including the correct one. Finally, everyone has to guess which is the real meaning—it can be surprisingly tricky!

CARL LINNAEUS, classification system, 1826

As well as arranging words in dictionaries, scholars also use words to organize information and knowledge. The Swedish botanist **Carl Linnaeus** (1707–1778) gave all living animals and plants two Latin names, by which they are still known today—a genus and a species. A tiger, for instance, is *Panthera tigris*, whereas a lion is *Panthera leo*. The shared word, *Panthera*, shows that both animals belong to a family of large cats that are able to roar. Today, we invent words for our new discoveries (stars, medicines) or for things that trouble us (hurricanes, diseases). Words help us make sense of our world!

Get the Message!

Languages work in different ways, and it's not always possible to translate something exactly. Sometimes the words just don't exist! In Russian, for example, there is a word for light blue and a word for dark blue, while in some languages, including Korean, the same word is used for blue and green. Does this mean that Russians and Koreans see colors differently? Some scientists believe it does!

Book translators have to search for the right words to use. The Harry Potter books have been translated into 79 languages and in each one the translator had to make sure that everything still made sense. In the French edition, Hogwarts is called "Poudlard," meaning "bacon lice"; in the Hebrew version, Sirius Black sings a Hannukah song instead of a Christmas one and in the Hindi, the magic spells are written in ancient Sanskrit instead of Latin.

There's a well-known phrase, "lost in translation," which means that the point of the original word or phrase has changed somewhere along the way, often because of a misunderstanding. When Italian astronomer *Giovanni Schiaparelli* (1835–1910) peered through a telescope at the surface of Mars in 1877 he described seas, continents and some dark lines he called channels (or "canali" in Italian). In English, this word is usually translated as "canals"—man-made waterways like the ones you find in cities such as Venice or Amsterdam. People got very excited at the idea that someone had built canals on Mars! Were they created by aliens—could there be life on Mars?

Sometimes words are very hard to explain in new languages. In Finnish, the old measurement "poronkusema" meant the distance a reindeer can travel before needing a bathroom break (around 4.6 miles)! However, the more we communicate with other people, the more words we share. Today, words like "pizza" and "sushi" are used all over the world—there's often no need for a translation at all.

PIZZA!

SUSHI!

53

5

POWERFUL WORDS

How words affect what we do

I'm Ashoka. I was emperor of the Indian Maurya Dynasty over 2,000 years ago. Stone pillars with my texts carved on them were placed around my kingdom. They gave people instructions for how to live their lives.

STOP GLOBAL WARMING

Other Worldly

For many of our ancient ancestors, words were a way of communicating with worlds beyond the human world. People gathered in groups to say prayers or sing songs that would connect them with their gods and ancestors. Today, ceremonies like the Maori's kapa haka, performed in Aotearoa, New Zealand, continue to be passed down through generations. Kapa haka song lyrics can be used to honor the dead, keep language and customs alive, and pass on traditions from one generation to the next.

Words became written instructions for how to live a good life. Some of the first words to be written down were the sacred texts of the world's religions—the Christian Bible, the Muslim Qu'ran, the Jewish Torah and the Hindu Vedas. The Old Testament Bible story tells of Moses bringing a stone down from Mount Sinai with ten rules or "commandments" carved on it. The commandments told the Hebrew people how they should live. Muslims follow a code known as the Pillars of Islam. A set of prayers, or "Salat," is performed five times a day, between dawn and midnight. Words hold great power for other religions and philosophies, too. Hindus and Buddhists recite words or phrases known as mantras while meditating.

ABRACADABRA
ABRACADABR
ABRACADAB
ABRACADA
ABRACAD
ABRACA
ABRAC
ABRA
ABR
AB
A

Magic Words

Do you recognize the word on this scrap of paper? You may have heard it in magic shows. Abracadabra has long been believed to have magic powers. This drawing is from the 2nd century book *Liber Medicinalis* (Book of Medicine) by the Roman doctor **Serenus Sammonicus** (d. 212 CE). The word was set out in this special way to form a triangle, with one letter removed at the end of each line. It was worn around the neck as a talisman—a protective charm designed to cure disease. It was thought that as the letters disappeared, so did the illness.

Can you think of any other magical words?
They might be old, too!

ABRACADABRA!

57

I HAVE A DREAM.

Inspiring Action

What words have inspired you? From thousand-year-old battle cries to famous quotations, words give us something to believe in. In 1963, in Washington, DC, *Martin Luther King Jr* (1929–1968) gave a speech often known by its first four words: "I have a dream." King's dream, that people should be judged by their actions and not by the color of their skin, still inspires us today.

It's through their words that people are often remembered. *Neil Armstrong* (1930–2012), the first man to walk on the moon, proclaimed as he stepped from the landing craft in 1969: "That's one small step for man. One giant leap for mankind." It's estimated that 600 million people across the world listened eagerly to those now-famous words as they were spoken 240,000 miles away in space.

THAT'S ONE SMALL STEP FOR MAN. ONE GIANT LEAP FOR MANKIND.

When you need people's support, it's important to choose the right words. In the UK, the suffragettes campaigned for women to be given the right to vote. Their slogan "Votes for Women!" appeared on badges, sashes, flags and banners from 1903. (They finally won the right to vote in 1918.) Their fight inspired a women's suffrage movement in the U.S., where the first women won the right to vote in 1920 with the 19th amendment to the U.S. Constitution. Throughout the 20th century, banners were held up in protests around the world, including "Wir sind ein Volk!" ("We are the People") at the Berlin Wall (1989). *Greta Thunberg's* (b. 2003) handwritten sign from 2018, "Skolstrejk för Klimatet" ("School Strike for Climate"), kickstarted a worldwide youth movement.

The invention of social media means that today words can be used to connect everyone, wherever they live in the world. By using the same hashtag (something first used in 2013), supporters of movements like "Black Lives Matter," which began in the U.S. in 2012, can link together— they don't have to protest in a particular place to feel part of a global movement. Social media gives them a platform where they can be heard.

Written into Law

If you and your friends were to write down something you all agreed to, and sign it, that document would be known as a contract. In this way, governments across the world turn words into laws. Laws are a set of rules that explain what we can or can't do. They are useful for settling arguments or dealing with bad behavior.

This was true even in the ancient world. In Mesopotamia, a set of laws known as the Code of Ur-Nammu (c. 2100 BCE) was written on clay tablets. In India, texts by *Emperor Ashoka the Great* (who reigned from c. 268–232 BCE)—with instructions for how to live a good, Buddhist life—were carved into large stone pillars. Today, we still say that something is "set in stone," when it can't easily be changed and will last for a long time.

Oaths are specially worded promises that are made in ceremonies, in front of others. You'll take an oath if you're being made Queen or President; if you're appearing in court as a witness; if you're getting married; or if you're becoming a citizen of a country. Doctors take the Hippocratic Oath, which dates back to the ancient Greek medic *Hippocrates* (410 BCE). They swear to treat patients to the best of their ability. Even magicians who are members of the Magic Circle must take a solemn vow never to give up the secrets of the tricks they've learned.

Color lithograph print of a magician, c. 1870–80.

Many banknotes also contain a written promise—one made by the bank to exchange the paper note for the sum of money described on it. Paper notes were first used back in Ming Dynasty China between 1375–1425 (a time when everyone else was using coins). They were larger than notes today, printed on mulberry bark paper, and came with a warning: "To counterfeit is death."

Piccadilly Circus, London, postcard c. 1955.

The Word on the Street

Next time you walk down a city street, you'll notice that words are everywhere. Walls have been carved and painted with words and letters ever since writing began. Painted text is still visible on the walls of Pompeii, the ancient Roman city that was buried under ash (and preserved in time) when the volcano Vesuvius erupted in 79 CE. Centuries later, when the printing press was invented, mass-produced posters were pasted next to painted signs and our streets could be filled with words even more quickly.

COOL

CAPS

If you walk down the street in Lagos, London or Las Vegas today, you will see hundreds of words staring out at you—signs offering directions, advertising products, describing shops, or offering advice. Huge billboards became popular in the U.S. from the 1830s; they were placed on top of buildings and at the roadside. The invention of electricity brought bigger, brighter signs, lit up with lights, which could be read from even further away. Once cars became popular in the early 20th century, signs sprang up everywhere, lining the new roads and highways.

Billboards and signs were useful for advertising products—and the advertising slogan was born. Slogans communicate in one simple phrase the idea behind a product or a brand, like Nike's "Just Do It!" or McDonald's "I'm Lovin' It." International companies understand the importance of words in getting a message across. If we can remember the phrase, and if it makes us feel happy or inspired, we're likely to connect the product (a pair of shoes, a burger meal) with that feeling too. All this through the power of words!

Words in Pictures

Today, artists from around the world use the streets as a canvas, leaving their "tag" in words and images. Graffiti comes from "graffiare," the Italian word meaning "to scratch," and the earliest forms of mark-making were the symbols and early letters scratched into stone caves underground—as long as 30,000 years ago. Graffiti tagging was a great craze in 1970s New York, where artists like **Lady Pink** (b. 1964) would spray-paint their names onto the many rundown buildings, walls and train carriages to show that they'd been there. **Jean-Michel Basquiat** (1960–1988), who started out as a graffiti artist, soon worked words, scratches and scribbles into his energetic drawings and paintings.

In the 20th century, artists were fascinated with words. **Pablo Picasso** (1881–1973) and **Georges Braque** (1882–1963) glued newspaper clippings into their paintings of 1912, and soon after, artists like **Hannah Höch** (1889–1978) worked cut-up snippets of text from magazines into her photographic collages. For these artists, using words showed that their art was connected to everyday life—instead of pictures from their imagination, their art included real things, taken from the real world.

ED RUSCHA, *OOF*, 1962

Since the 1960s the American artist **Ed Ruscha** (b. 1937) has also made paintings using words, and many of them celebrate the power of words themselves. He started out as a sign painter while at art school in Los Angeles. Works like *OOF* (1962, above), show how much he enjoys the shape as well as the sound of words. Words are eye-catching—we just can't help looking at them!

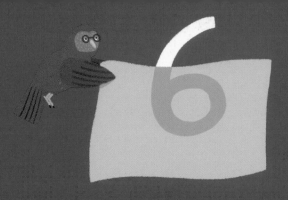

6

SECRET WORDS
Hiding and revealing the meaning of words

I'm Jean-François Champollion. In 1822 I deciphered Egyptian hieroglyphs on the ancient Rosetta Stone. My work paved the way for a greater understanding of this ancient language.

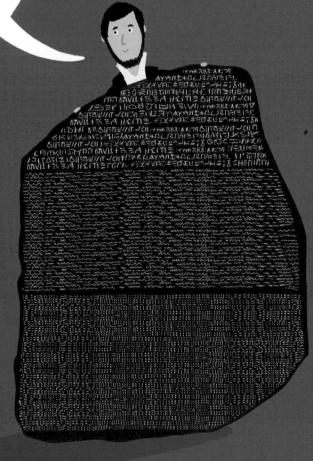

Get Cracking!

Have you ever cracked a code?

Much of what we know about the past is thanks to the skills of code breakers. Back in 1799, a 4,000-year-old chunk of rock known as the Rosetta Stone was discovered in Rosetta, Egypt. It contained a text (about King Ptolemy V) written three times, in different scripts: Egyptian hieroglyphs, Egyptian script and ancient Greek. The code was cracked by French linguist **Jean-François Champollion** (1790–1832) in 1822. For the first time, it was possible to decipher Egyptian hieroglyphs (a "cipher" is another word for a code).

Codes can be used to disguise words as well as reveal them! If you need to send a secret message, there are many types of code you can use. Morse Code is a series of dots, dashes and spaces that replace the A to Z letters of the alphabet. It was invented in 1838 at the same time as the electric telegraph, one of the earliest machines that could transmit sound across long distances. As long as the receiver knew the code, they could understand the messages communicated by short beeps (for dots) and longer sounds (for dashes).

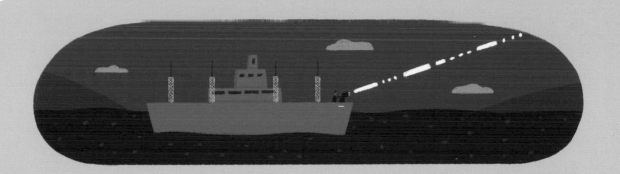

At sea, messages in Morse could also be transmitted by flashlight—quick flashes for dots and long glares for dashes. Like many codes, Morse involved a simple swap—one letter for one symbol. Other codes (which you could try out yourself) involve using numbers or symbols to represent words and letters. Turn to page 93 for some ideas!

In wartime, inventing (and cracking) codes was important work, and with the invention of machines, codes became more complicated. During World War II at Bletchley Park, UK, a team of people designed and programmed powerful code-breaking machines, including a huge contraption called the Bombe. It was invented by *Alan Turing* (1912–1954) and operated by members of the Women's Royal Naval Service, known as the "Wrens," including *Jean Valentine* (1924–2019). With it, they decoded thousands of messages containing secret enemy plans.

Word Play

Word games are as old as words themselves!
The Romans created a grid of words known as the Sator Square—
a 5 x 5 letter grid containing five words that read up, down, forwards
and backwards. It has been found on ancient buildings from the
earliest example in Pompeii to places as far apart as Syria and Sweden.
Even though its five Latin words can be read clearly, scholars have
puzzled for centuries over its exact meaning and have suggested many
different interpretations, from Christian prayers to magical charms.

Riddles—baffling questions that leave you scratching your head—
can also be traced back to ancient times. This riddle is a shortened
version of one written in cuneiform on a 4,000-year-old tablet:

There is a house. One enters it blind and leaves it seeing. What is it?

Greek legend also tells of the voyager Oedipus, who attempted to
solve the riddle of the Sphinx, the mythical creature with the head
of a human and the body of a lion, said to have guarded the gate
to the ancient city of Thebes:

What creature has one voice, but has four feet in the morning, two feet in the afternoon and three feet at night?

During the 20th century word games became more popular as the number of printed books, magazines and newspapers increased. The crossword puzzle, first devised by **Arthur Wynne** (1871–1945) in 1913 for the Sunday pages of a New York newspaper, swept the world as a craze soon afterwards, while the game Scrabble, invented by architect **Alfred Butts** (1899–1993) in the U.S. in 1933, is played all over the world. If you have a set, you could try making your own version of the Sator Square!

If you have great powers of observation, you might be able to unscramble words by looking at them carefully. Can you (and your friends!) solve this anagram (a puzzle where the letters are rearranged):

OH FOR FRESH DICTIONARY WORLDS

You'll find the answers on page 93.
You could invent some of your own, too!

Invented Languages

We've thought about making up codes, disguising and revealing words—but word play can also involve inventing completely new languages. Sometimes, these creations can be very personal, not intended to be seen by anyone else. Back in the 12th century, musician and writer **Hildegard of Bingen** (1098–1179 CE) invented her own language that only she could understand.

Detail of a miniature painting showing Hildegard of Bingen at a writing desk.

Studies of twins have also shown they sometimes dream up unusual ways of communicating with each other—an invented language between twins is known as "cryptophasia" (from "crypto" meaning "secret" and "phasia" meaning "speech").

There are also languages invented just for stories, like the language spoken by the Elves in *J. R. R. Tolkien's Lord of the Rings* (1954) or the language Klingon spoken by a race of aliens in the science-fiction series *Star Trek*. Klingon was written by linguist *Marc Okrand* (b. 1948), and today it even has its own mode in the language app Duolingo! Creating a language is a great challenge for someone who likes rules, poetry and math. Writer, poet and mathematician *Daniel Tammet* (b. 1979) created one such language called "Mänti."

Other playful experiments with words and languages you could try include the lipogram—a piece of writing in which all words containing a particular letter have been deliberately left out. The French author *Georges Perec* (1936–1982) wrote the book *La Disparition* in 1969, a text that didn't include the letter E (the French language's most commonly used letter). This was also a challenge for his English translator, *Gilbert Adair* (1944–2011), who had to translate it without using the letter E, too! His English translation is called *A Void*.

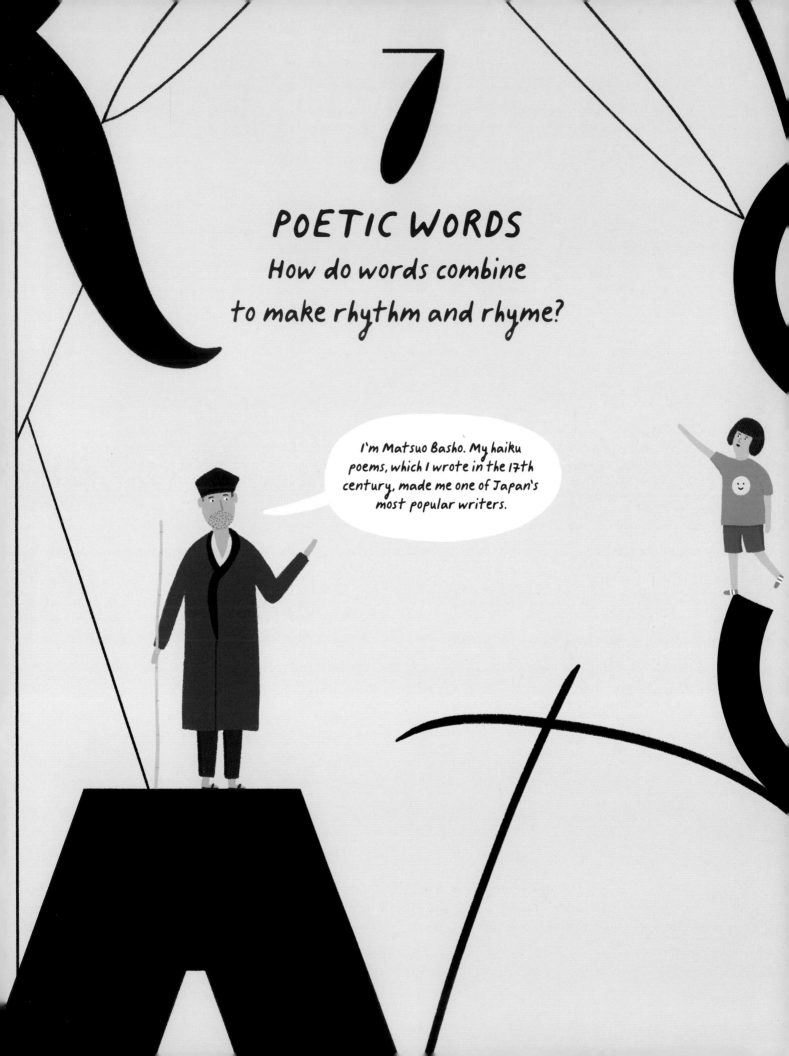

POETIC WORDS
How do words combine to make rhythm and rhyme?

I'm Matsuo Basho. My haiku poems, which I wrote in the 17th century, made me one of Japan's most popular writers.

Writing Poems

The poet *Emily Dickinson* (1830–1886) once wrote: "I know nothing in the world that has as much power as a word. Sometimes I write one, and I look at it, until it begins to live." She used her own powerful words to write nearly 1,800 poems, which were often about nature. She hardly ever left her house in Amherst, Massachusetts, but her poems show that her life was very rich and full of meaning. Even today—about 150 years later—when we read a poem by Emily Dickinson, her words and ideas come alive again in our minds.

Aren't words amazing? A poem is an example of a piece of writing where every single word matters. You wouldn't want to swap one word for another—because every one of them is playing an important part, like a tower of balancing acrobats. Changing just one word might alter the whole poem.

The words in a poem often bring many things to mind at once; they get our brains working. Choose a word—let's say "winter." Without thinking too hard, say what pops into your head. You might think of trees without leaves, frosty mornings, or crunchy snow. Well, that's what your brain's doing when you see a word in a poem. All your "winter" thoughts start whirring away, as you work out what the poem means to you.

Impression of a seal from the Akkadian period, Iraq, c. 2254–2193 BCE

We know that our ancestors started writing poetry long ago—
on page 24 we heard about the Akkadian princess **Enheduanna**'s
poems that were carved in the stone walls of the Temple of Ur 4,000
years ago. Long ago, only rulers, scholars or priests knew how to read.
But everyone could learn to recite poems, prayers and songs from
memory. If you've ever tried to remember a poem, you've probably
noticed that rhythms or rhymes (and in songs, tunes) make lines of
poetry much easier to remember. The epic, ancient tales of Homer
didn't rhyme—but they followed a strict meter—in poetry, that's
the rhythm in which the words are spoken.

Word Patterns

There are two main things to think about when you're looking at a poem. There's the **content** (what the poem's about) and the **form** (the sound of the words the poet has chosen, and the poem's rhythm and rhyming patterns). When you're writing, it can be helpful to follow a set of rules to give your poem shape.

A limerick is a poem with a very predictable rhyming pattern. Take this one by the English artist and poet *Edward Lear* (1812–1888):

There was an Old Man with a beard,
Who said, "It is just as I feared!—
Two Owls and a Hen, four Larks and a Wren,
Have all built their nests in my beard."

EDWARD LEAR, *There was an Old Man with a beard...*, 1846

If you replace the actual words with these sounds, and clap along, you can hear the rhythm even more clearly:

De da-da de da-da de dur // De da-da de da-da de dur
De da da da dah // De da da da dah
De da-da de da-da de dur

7. Poetic Words

Let's take a very different example. A **haiku** is a poem made up of three separate, but connected, phrases. In the original Japanese, haikus are made up of a total of 17 syllables (5 in the first part, then 7, then 5). A syllable is one sound (the word "totaling" has three syllables: *to-tal-ing*). Haikus by *Basho* (1644–1694), like this one from 1686, were often inspired by nature and his travels to the countryside:

an ancient pond / a frog jumps in / the splash of water
furu ike ya / kawazu tobikomu / mizu no oto
古池や蛙飛び込む水の音
ふるいけやかわずとびこむみずのおと

PLOP

Poems don't *have* to follow any rules, of course! But poets will always pay special attention to the sound of words. When you read poems aloud, look out for **alliteration** (when words begin with the same letter or sound: "Peter Piper picked a peck of pickled peppers"). You might also spot examples of **onomatopoeia**, a wonderful word that means that the word in question sounds like the thing it's describing (Pop! Meow! Buzz!).

Spoken Word

If you really want to enjoy the words you're looking at on a page—read them aloud. Poems in the past were often sung, accompanied by musicians. Today, rappers and spoken-word poets deliver rhymes against a beat or backing track.

Rap became popular in New York in the late 1970s. In a piece of rap, MCs (which stands for "master of ceremonies" or "microphone controller") rhyme over the music. Rapping freestyle is to improvise, or make up rhymes on the spot—you don't know exactly what you're going to say in advance. **Lin-Manuel Miranda** (b. 1980), author of the stage musical *Hamilton* (2015), started out as a rap improvisor, and turned those early ideas into songs that told stories. In 2009, at an event at the White House (in front of then-President Barack Obama and Michelle Obama) Miranda performed a rap about the 18th-century American politician Alexander Hamilton. Out of this, *Hamilton*, a musical delivered entirely in rhyme, was born.

"Rap battles" or "poetry slams" are popular ways for rappers and poets to compete with each other. *Prince of Poets*, a show broadcast on Abu Dhabi TV, is a poetry competition where people compete to be crowned champion rhymer. It's named after the Egyptian poet **Ahmed Shawqi** (1868–1932), who was known as the "prince of poets" in his time.

Ask a friend to pick a subject. See if you can make up a poem or a rap on the spot! First, you'll have to take a moment to collect your thoughts and prepare what you're going to say. You could perform to a beat, which will help you keep going and give you a structure for your words as they flow out. Freestyle rappers who take part in competitions often plan a few rhymes or word patterns in advance. You could create some lists of your favorite rhymes, in case you need to use them!

THE LAST WORD
What's the future of words?

I'm the British scientist Stephen Hawking. My discoveries about black holes changed the way we think about space. In 1985 I lost the use of my voice due to illness, but I was still able to speak using a computer program connected to a digital voice box.

Languages in Danger!

Languages are kept alive by people using them every day. Just like rare animals in deserts or rainforests, some languages are also endangered and face extinction. A language dies when its last speaker does, and it's estimated that a third of the world's c. 7,000 languages have fewer than 1,000 speakers left.

Why might that be? Today, we're more connected with our siblings around the world than ever before. And commonly spoken languages are incredibly useful for living, working and learning—so the most popular ones are then spoken by more and more people.

In 1887 **L. L. Zamenhof** (1859–1917) from Poland decided to invent a totally new language called Esperanto. He designed it using simple rules so that people could learn it quickly. He thought that if everyone learned to speak it (along with their original language), people around the world could be united. Although many people do still speak Esperanto, it didn't become as popular as he'd hoped!

Marie Wilcox (1933–2021), a member of the Wukchumni tribe in California, was the last fluent speaker of Wukchumni when she decided to save the language from extinction. She taught the language and worked for 20 years on a Wukchumni dictionary, using computer technology and sound recording to help her.

Indigenous languages are those spoken by the people who lived in a land before colonization (when one country invades another and claims leadership of it and the people who live there). Learning an indigenous language is a way of acknowledging those people and the land's history. The UNESCO Atlas of Languages in Danger, founded in 1996, records where certain languages are still spoken. On its website (see page 93), you can look up a country's rare languages, and find out roughly how many people still speak them. Charities encourage governments to revive and record these ancient languages so that they are not lost forever. For example, on Easter Island (Rapa Nui), an island in the Pacific Ocean, school children are learning their native Rapa Nui language so that it will live on.

With a lot of effort, it's possible to bring languages back to life. For centuries, the ancient language Hebrew was used by the Jewish people only in religious ceremonies and sacred books. It wasn't used in daily life until it was revived in the 19th and 20th centuries. Linguists added new words, and today it's spoken by around 9 million people worldwide. There's always hope for a language!

A World Wide Web

Whatever language you speak—whether it's Portuguese, Polish or Persian—new words appear and old ones disappear every year. The world is always changing, and words to describe new trends, inventions, ideas or expressions have to change with it. Today, you might be using words or phrases that didn't even exist last year; there's no way of telling what new ones you'll be using next year!

Our ways of writing to each other change too. The internet, invented in 1983, started out as a way of helping libraries and universities share information. Soon, it connected people around the globe, and today half the world's population is online. Technology shapes the words we use, and the way we use them. From the telegram—a method of messaging popular in the 1920s and 30s, where people had to communicate in short sentences (because they were paying by the word)—to the text message (with its popular abbreviations like LOL or OMG), humans are used to squeezing their words into many different kinds of messages!

Emojis designed by O'Plérou Grebet

Sometimes we message without using words at all. The emoji, first used in 1997, was developed by Japanese designer *Shigetaka Kurita* (b. 1972). Emoji means "picture character" in Japanese. Emojis can also help the person you're texting interpret your words! We often use emojis that reflect our everyday lives. So when the Ivorian designer *O'Plérou Grebet* (b. 1997) realized many aspects of West African culture weren't reflected in standard emojis, he decided to make his own. He has designed more than 365 emojis showing African culture.

It's estimated that 6 billion emojis are sent around the world every day. An emoji is more like a sign than a word—perhaps it's even something our ancient ancestors would understand!

Computer Language

Since the invention of computers (as we know them today) in the 1950s and the internet in 1983, technology has come a long way. Computers can perform complicated tasks at faster and faster speeds. They power machines that can solve problems or carry out actions in the same way that humans would. This is known as AI, or "artificial intelligence." In 1997, IBM's Deep Blue computer beat the chess champion *Garry Kasparov* (b. 1963)—a feat that seemed impossible just a decade before.

Computers can also be programmed to assist humans in particular ways. The scientist *Stephen Hawking* (1942–2018) lost the use of many of his muscles due to illness, but was able to speak and write again thanks to a computer program he operated by twitching the muscles in his cheek. He was celebrated for his work in expanding our understanding of how the universe works, and for his communication skills—he delivered lectures, made public appearances and wrote bestselling science books that sold millions of copies.

oloollll olllolll ollollloo oolooooo
olloooool olloillo ollooloo oolooooo
ollloili olloilli ollloooolo olloiloi oolooooo
olllolli olloolol ollloooolo olloolol oolooooo
olloioooo olloolol ollloooolo olloolol

Today, computers are more powerful than ever. They speak to each other in their own language, called code. They use algorithms (sets of instructions for the computer to follow) to sift and sort information, or "data." Every day, billions of words are typed into search engines, like Google, which scan a database of billions more words to dig out the facts and figures we're looking for. Through Google Translate, and other language software programs, we can instantly translate one language into another. We are quite used to having virtual assistants on our smartphones and in our homes that respond to voice commands, digital phone operators that can understand our voices and bots that can respond to questions online.

The next chapter in our history of words hasn't been written yet, but computers will certainly play a part. We know that they can do amazing things. Thanks to their ability to recognize patterns and crack codes, they can help doctors to understand the way diseases spread or scholars to decode ancient languages. We need to make sure we continue to put the amazing technology we've invented to good use, using our words—and our human skills of working together, understanding and caring for each other—to help make the world a better place.

PLAY "OWL SONGS!'

TIMELINE OF THE HISTORY OF WORDS

BCE stands for "Before the Common Era"
CE stands for "Common Era"
c. stands for "circa" and means approximately

Historians originally thought that Jesus was born in the year 1, at the start of the Common Era. Events that occurred before his birth are counted back from that year, and events after his birth are counted forwards. When it is obvious a date is in the Common Era, the letters CE are not used.

AT LEAST 2 MILLION YEARS AGO

Early humans communicate with each other through shared sounds and signs. This is the beginning of language.

200,000 YEARS AGO

Our ancestors, Homo sapiens, start using language in more complex ways, and by c. 50,000 BCE are using it to invent and share stories.

FROM c. 3400 BCE

The Sumerian people begin the cuneiform system of writing with wedge-shaped symbols in clay. It is used for business, stories and poems.

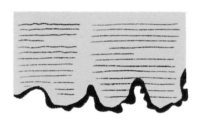

c. 300 BCE

The Dead Sea Scrolls are written in Hebrew script on papyrus, animal skins and copper. They contain the oldest known version of the Bible.

c. 285-246 BCE

The Great Library of Alexandria is founded in Egypt. It holds books and scrolls of literature, mathematics, philosophy and science.

c. 300 BCE

The Mayan system of writing is developed in Mesoamerica. Made up of 800 symbols, it is carved onto stone slabs, sculptures and pottery.

1604

The first English dictionary is published by Robert Cawdrey. In 1755, Samuel Johnson publishes a dictionary containing 40,000 words.

1700-1800

More people learn to read and books and newspapers become cheaper. Novels become popular as people start to read for pleasure.

1799

The Rosetta Stone is discovered in Egypt. Carved with three ancient scripts, experts use it to translate hieroglyphic writing.

FROM c. 3200 BCE

The Egyptians carve hieroglyphics onto the walls of temples and tombs, including spells to help the dead on their journey to the afterlife.

c. 1600–c. 1050 BCE

In Shang Dynasty China, spells and prophecies are written on animal bones and are the earliest surviving records of the Chinese alphabet.

FROM c. 1000 BCE

The Phoenicians invent an alphabet of 22 letters that combine to form words. This becomes the Greek alphabet, which we still use today.

c. 100 BCE

Paper is invented in China and in 800 CE text is printed on paper using carved wooden blocks. Now a text can be copied many times over.

c. 800 CE

Calligraphy is used to turn handwritten Arabic script into beautiful works of art. Text from the Qu'ran is decorated with gold.

1440s

Johannes Gutenberg invents the printing press, in Germany. Thousands of copies of books can be printed at once.

FROM 1867

The invention of the typewriter makes it possible for people to write more quickly and for what they write to be easy for people to read.

1940s

During World War II computer engineers race to invent machines that are capable of cracking secret wartime codes.

1983

The internet is invented and in 1989 the world wide web connects people from around the world. People can share their work and ideas for free.

GLOSSARY

ALGORITHM a set of rules for a computer to follow in order to follow a task or solve a problem.

ALLITERATION the use of the same sound at the beginning of several words that are close together.

CUNEIFORM a form of writing in wedge-shaped characters used for over 3,000 years in the ancient countries of Mesopotamia.

CALLIGRAPHY the art of doing beautiful writing using special pens or brushes.

GRAMMAR the set of rules that explains how words are used in a language.

HAIKU a type of Japanese poem that has three lines and a certain number of syllables on each line—five, then seven, then five.

HIEROGLYPH a symbol or picture that represents a word. Used in some writing systems, such as the one used in ancient Egypt.

INCANTATION a series of words that are believed to have a magical effect when spoken or sung.

INSCRIBE to carve or cut words on an object.

LIPOGRAM a piece of writing from which all words containing a particular letter have been deliberately left out.

LIMERICK a humorous rhyming poem with five lines and a strong rhythm.

LINGUIST a person who studies and speaks a lot of languages.

MANUSCRIPT a book or document. Often refers to very old books and documents that were written by hand before printing was invented.

MANTRA a word, sound or phrase that is repeated as a prayer. In the Hindu and Buddhist religions, people speak mantras to help with meditation.

ONOMATOPOEIA the use of words that sound like the noise they refer to. "Thud," "boom" and "hiss" are all examples of onomatopoeia.

PAPYRUS a type of paper made from the stems of the papyrus plant. It was used in ancient Egypt, Rome and Greece.

PARCHMENT the skin of an animal that was stretched thin and dried, then used to write on.

PUBLISH to produce and sell a book, magazine or newspaper. When a publishing company publishes a book, it prints copies of it and sends them to stores to be sold.

SCHOLAR a person who studies a subject and knows a lot about it.

SCROLL a long roll of paper with writing on it. Information was stored on scrolls in the ancient world.

SCRIBE a person who copied letters and documents by hand in times before printing was common.

SCRIPT a particular system of writing with letters or symbols. A script is also the written text for a play or film.

SLOGAN a short, attention-grabbing phrase that is used to advertise a product or an idea.

STYLUS a tool made from wood, metal or bone, used in ancient times for writing on clay or wax tablets. A stylus was pointed at one end for writing, and blunt at the other for erasing marks.

SYLLABLE one of the sounds into which a word can be separated. Each syllable usually has a vowel (a, e, i, o or u). "Girl" has one syllable, "woman" has two.

TABLET a piece of wood covered with a layer of soft wax or clay that could be written on with a pointed tool called a stylus.

TRANSLATION a piece of writing or speech that has been changed, or translated, from one language into another.

SOURCES

There are enough books about the history of words and language to fill whole libraries! I've loved dipping into books I've had on my shelves, books in libraries, articles online, and TV documentaries, too. In particular, I've enjoyed:

BOOKS

Bellos, David. *Is That a Fish in Your Ear? The Amazing Adventure of Translation*. London: Penguin Books, 2012.

Casely-Hayford, Gus (au., ed.), Topp Fargion, Janet (ed.) and Wallace, Marion (ed.). *West Africa: Word, Symbol, Song*. London: The British Library Publishing Division, 2015.

Eagleton, Terry. *How to Read a Poem*. Malden: Blackwell, 2012.

Fischer, Steven Roger. *A History of Reading*. New edition. London: Reaktion Books, 2019.

Harari, Yuval Noah. *Sapiens: A Brief History of Humankind*. London: Harvill Secker, 2014.

Morley, Simon. *Writing on the Wall: Word and Image in Modern Art*. London: Thames & Hudson, 2007.

Robinson, Andrew. *The Story of Writing: Alphabets, Hieroglyphs and Pictograms*. London: Thames & Hudson, 2007.

ShaoLan. *Chineasy: The New Way to Read Chinese*. London: Thames & Hudson, 2014.

Wolf, Maryanne. *Proust and the Squid: The Story and Science of the Reading Brain*. New York: Harper Perennial, 2017.

PODCASTS & WEBSITES

Rosen, Michael. "Word of Mouth." BBC Radio Four. 1992–present.

UNESCO Atlas of the World's Languages in Danger. unesco.org/languages-atlas/index.php?hl=en&page=atlasmap [last accessed: 01/02/2022]

TV & FILM

Davidson, John Paul (dir.), Fry, Stephen (writer and presenter). *Fry's Planet Word*. United Kingdom: BBC Two, 2011.

Sington, David (dir.). *The Secret History of Writing*. United Kingdom: BBC Four, 2020.

ANSWERS

Speaking My Language (page 46)

The word **language** is French in origin—it's based on the Latin word "lingua," meaning "tongue." **Thousand** is Old English, based on the German word "tausend." **Paragraph** is based on the Greek "paragraphos" ("a short line marking a break in sense") and is derived from "para," meaning "beside," and "graphos," meaning "write"—while **fascinating** is based on the Latin word "fascinat," which means "bewitched." You can look up other words, too!

Get Cracking! (page 69)

A simple code is one where you substitute one letter for another. For example, write out the alphabet (A to Z). Underneath each letter, write the letter you're going to swap it for—let's say A–C, B–D, C–E, D–F... and so on.

If you wanted to write the word "BAD," you'd instead write "DCF"—and only a friend with the key to your code would be able to understand you!

Word Play (page 70-71)

Q: There is a house. One enters it blind and leaves it seeing. What is it?
A: A school.

Q: What creature has one voice, but has four feet in the morning, two feet in the afternoon and three feet at night?
A: A person! (Four feet in the morning = crawling on hands and feet as a baby; two feet in the afternoon = walking on two legs as a child and adult; three feet at night = walking with the help of a cane as an elderly person.)

Q: Can you solve this anagram?
OH FOR FRESH DICTIONARY WORLDS
A: A HISTORY OF WORDS FOR CHILDREN

LIST OF ILLUSTRATIONS

Dimensions are given in centimeters, followed by inches

INDEX

I'd like to dedicate this book to all the wonderful authors who have
ever sat in front of their tablet, parchment, paper or keyboard and
created something for the world to read. It's also for David, Arlo,
Zubin, Quincy and Viola Schweitzer who all have a brilliant way
with words. And it's for Chuckle—thanks for the alarm call!—M.R.

A History of Words for Children © 2022 Thames & Hudson Ltd, London
Text © 2022 Mary Richards
Illustrations © 2022 Rose Blake

Consultant Vinod Aithal

First published in 2022 in the United States of America by
Thames & Hudson Inc., 500 Fifth Avenue, New York, New York 10110

Library of Congress Control Number 2021952544

ISBN 978-0-500-65282-4

Printed in China by Shanghai Offset Printing Products Limited

Be the first to know about our new releases,
exclusive content and author events by visiting
thamesandhudson.com
thamesandhudsonusa.com
thamesandhudson.com.au